LIFE AFTER LOSS FOR WIDOWS:

Lifting the Veil of Grief

PEGGY BELL

Facebook: liveyourpurposelifecoaching
Lifeafterlossforwidows
Instagram: live_yourpurpose
Email: peggybellwrites@yahoo.com

Disclaimer: This book is not intended to diagnose or cure anyone who is
having an extremely difficult time with grief. It was written to share my
difficulties with grief and how I recovered from them. Its purpose was to
let women know they are not alone in the journey.

DEDICATION

I dedicate this book to all women who have had to face the reality of losing their spouse.

You too, in time, can leave the darkness of your cocoon and become the radiant butterfly you deserve to become.

CONTENTS

PREFACE

Grief stinks. Anyone going through it will certainly understand and most likely agree. Grief does not discriminate. It delivers an emotional suffering that takes its toll on you. It is personal and you must endure it to get through it. It is the price we pay for loving someone. It takes a good amount of energy and exertion to live again in the present without dwelling on the past. The upside, if there is one, is that you *can* get through it. I know, because it happened to me.

Grief is associated with different types of losses in our lives, such as the loss of a marriage, a child, a parent, a home, or even a job. For purposes of this book, we will be concentrating with the type of grief associated with the loss of a husband. I want to talk about women who find themselves with the unwanted title of *widow.*

This book is written from my perspective about two words I now despise- *loss* and *grief*. The pain and the loneliness I felt was the worst I ever experienced. I was always interested in self-improvement reading. Over the years, I attended trainings and read books about reaching new heights and getting the things we want in life, but I never read or learned about dealing with people we love and lose.

Going through grief can make you feel so lonely and isolated. It is my wish that if you can identify with any of this, you will know you are not alone. It is not uncommon in the way you feel. People experience many of these emotions.

I did not want this book to be only about darkness and gloom. I want you to know that by the end of this book you can feel hopeful that better days are ahead. You may not be able to see the light at the end of the dark tunnel just yet, but rest assured there *is* a light waiting for you. There can be a transition to recovery on the other side of grief. It is not something you ever get over, but it is something you can get through.

This book intends to show the vulnerable, authentic side from someone who walked the walk and who talks the talk with others on a daily basis. I worded it as though I were talking to a friend because, in some sort of way, we are friends. We have experienced the loss of our soul mate, the person we did not choose to let go of so soon. That connects us through this common bond. It sort of makes us part of a sisterhood. Unless you have gone through it, it's difficult to comprehend the magnitude of the hurt which one feels. It affects parts of our lives we did not even consider. I compare it as going from wearing a wedding veil of marriage, where everything is bright and happy and you're looking forward to a great future, to wearing a widow's veil of grief, where it is difficult to see anything beyond the darkness of the present, much less the future.

The book begins with my story and how I came to know about the pain associated with such a loss. I was thrown into a *club* where I did not choose to become a member. If you picked up this book, chances are you are a club member as well, or you are giving it to someone who is. Maybe you are reading it to better understand what widows face during their time of loss. It will pinpoint certain areas that were especially difficult for me to handle. I shared what each area was and how I handled it (or was unable to handle it). It starts from the beginning and moves through the emotional journey. My objective is for this to truly be a self-growth book, a "companion" if you will, to have with you when you need the assurance that you are not alone through this very difficult time in your life.

"Your love for me could not be measured in weight, but rather by the way you made me feel."

Peggy Bell

Section One
My Story

August 25, 2009, was the day that unraveled not just me, but my whole world. It was the day life, as I knew it, would never again be the same. Randy, my husband of thirty years, passed from this world that day. The love of my life, the father of our children, my soulmate, best friend and confidant, took his last breath. His earthly journey was finished.

Randy had been ill for a while. He had diabetes and suffered from many of the ailments that wicked disease commonly causes. I knew in my heart that he wouldn't live to see an old age, but I was not ready for it to happen so soon. Neither was he. In fact, he had seen two of his doctors just the week before. The first was his cardiologist. He told us there was no change in his recent heart tests. We were told to return in six months. The second was his family doctor. He told Randy at that particular visit he thought he would have about ten more years of life. Randy was the one who had asked the doctor and was excited to hear that news. We all were. Sadly, they could not have been more wrong. He died about seven days later. When that sweet man passed, so did a huge part of me. I was married to him for more than half of my life. Through the years, we molded as one, always together, always laughing, and always holding hands every time we sat next to each other. It was just something that felt natural. We were there for each other in good times and in bad, in sickness and in health, until death did us part. He was not perfect, but he was perfect for me. Losing him made my heart slowly bleed out and wither, never again to be revived to its original state.

That day still replays in my mind after all these years. I often think about the last words that we spoke to each other that morning. I wish they would have been romantic and poetic like the death scenes you see on television but they weren't. He asked me how I was feeling as I was getting ready for work and I answered, "the same." (I was recovering from knee surgery.) He turned over and went back to sleep. I left for work. Those words, though nothing fancy, will stick with me forever. They were *our* last words.

Randy died at home about three hours later as close as we can tell. My daughter found him and called me. I raced home. Luckily, the campus where I taught was only a mile and a half from where we lived so I arrived before the ambulance. I tried to revive him, but I knew it was too late. The emergency technician confirmed it after he examined him.

From that moment on, the day, (as well as my life for a long time), was a blur. My house quickly filled with several emergency technicians, a few police officers, the coroner who was there to ask me questions, and the funeral director. I answered all of their questions as best as I could. At least I think I did. I do not even remember if I cried. I was in shock and disbelief. The man I dearly loved had just died and I *do not even remember if I cried*. Phone calls were made to family and close friends. Someone announced it on social media. Our pastor came and spoke to my daughters and me. A couple of my daughters' best friends came by as well as my own. Though deeply appreciated, I honestly do not remember our conversations. My mind was tossed into a dense sea of fog with no signs of clearing.

I wanted to be strong for my two daughters. Even though they were both in their twenties, we were a very close family and they were devastated and hurting as well. They did not need to be worried about me. Their plate was full. There were big changes happening in our family. Our older daughter was engaged to be married in four and a half months. Our younger daughter was scheduled to leave home in two days. She was transferring to another college away from home for the first time. Randy and I had been preparing ourselves for *empty nest syndrome* most parents go through. I could not let my girls down. I was their only parent now and I had to be their pillar of strength. I had no idea how I would do it, but I knew I had to somehow.

I remember going to bed that first night. Randy had been in the hospital many times before. He had been in poor health for years so I often slept alone on those nights that I wasn't staying at the hospital. This time, however, I knew he was not coming home from the hospital. He was not coming home, period. The empty place on that side of our bed was now my cruel reality. I left for work that morning as a married woman and returned three hours later as a widow. How does anyone make sense of that? I held on to his pillow and cried harder than I had all day. My chest was tight and I could barely breathe. The pillow was wet from so many tears. At some point I fell asleep because I awoke to see daylight.

It was a new day, but it was so very bleak. We had to make funeral arrangements. How does one truly prepare herself to make funeral arrangements for someone you never wanted to lose? My sister in law and her husband came in from out of state to be there for us and to help in any way they could.

One of the good things about being a close-knit family is that it was easy to agree on arrangements without any unnecessary drama. I was thankful we did not have it, but I was not expecting any. It was a little difficult getting around due to my recent knee surgery, but I made it through the day of planning. The funeral would be three days away so all of our extended family and close friends from out of state could make it in on the weekend. The days that followed consisted of friends stopping by, bringing food, and offering their sympathy. We were not alone much during that time. My younger daughter made arrangements and received permission to start school a little later. She wanted to stay home with me and change her plans of going to school out of town. I loved her for even considering it but insisted she keep her plans. I gave my older daughter the choice if she wanted to postpone the wedding or not. I told her she did not have to and her dad wouldn't expect her to do so. My husband and I were blessed with two thoughtful daughters who were a joy to parent as young girls and an even greater joy to have as grown young women. After much talk and consideration, each agreed to stick to their original plans for their futures and it was fine with me. Deep inside, I knew the day they each left would be another kick in the gut, but the last thing I wanted was for them to alter their plans because of me. I would only feel worse in the end.

The church was filled with family and friends on the day of the funeral. I did not want a sanitized portrayal of my husband. I wanted to celebrate the life of who he genuinely was. Selected friends and coworkers spoke during the service. They told stories that made us laugh and stories that made us cry. Randy was quite a character and always had funny stories to tell. What was always so funny was the fact that those stories were real. He always managed to find himself in the most peculiar and hilarious situations. That, along with his kind heart and outgoing personality, is what people remembered and loved most about him. We believed he had the type of service he would have wanted. By the end of the day, we were drained, both mentally and physically. It had been a very long week.

I took a little time off from teaching. The following two weeks consisted of tending to finances and legal matters, buying a headstone, writing thank you notes, and keeping busy with other things that made the days go by rather quickly. There were times when I stopped and cried. This was mostly while writing the thank you notes. The nights however, were a different story. They remained excruciating. I had time on my hands at night to think about my loss. Reality hit me in the face each time I entered our bedroom. A wave of panic and deeper sadness sank into the pit of my stomach while getting into bed each night. I missed him so much and I wanted him back more than anything I had ever wanted in my life. Like every other night since his passing, I hugged his pillow and cried myself to sleep off and on throughout the night.

My older daughter lived at home until the wedding. Shortly after the funeral, time came for my younger daughter to move away to begin a new semester in college at her new school. I remember that day. She drove and moved herself. She had a roommate waiting for her when she arrived to help her unpack. I was still struggling to walk for long periods of time so I could not help to get her moved. I tried to be strong when she hugged me goodbye in the driveway. I knew she had mixed emotions of her own and I did not want to upset her by crying. I remember seeing her car drive away. I watched until I no longer saw her. I walked into the kitchen, stopped halfway, grabbed hold of the countertop and wailed. For the first time since losing my husband I was completely alone in the house and was able to let out my emotions at will. I guess I needed that more than I even realized. I cried until I could not cry anymore.

Two months after the funeral I found out I needed yet another knee surgery. Apparently, I had torn the cartilage again while trying to revive my husband that day. My daughter's wedding was in two months. There were lots to do and lots of recovery if I did not want to be on crutches for the wedding. Thankfully, goals were accomplished on both accounts.

The wedding was lovely but it was also bittersweet. There was still so much raw emotion in all of us. It had only been four and a half months since he was gone. My husband would have loved to be there to walk his first-born daughter down the aisle. He was looking forward to it and had made special, fun plans for it. She asked Randy's best friend if he would fill in for her dad. To our surprise, we were told that Randy had already asked him to do that just in case anything happened to him. We were happy to follow out his wishes. There was a memorial table to honor his memory. Both daughters and I placed a long stem white rose by his picture and memorial candle when we approached the front of the aisle. Many tears were shed that night, but just as all the days before, we got through it somehow.

I returned to teaching after being off from the surgery and tried to get back into the routine I was used to. It wasn't easy but I was really trying. I was living alone for the first time in my life. I went from being someone's daughter and living at home with my parents and sisters, straight to being someone's wife and then someone's mother. Living alone in a house was a foreign concept. There were reminders of Randy and our life together everywhere. Our home felt lonely and unusually quiet. I did not like it. I found myself coming home from work in the afternoons, eating a quick bite, taking a shower, and being in bed before it was even dark out just to end the days. I hated my life. I was emotionally withdrawn from people. I had no desire to watch television or to read. I just wanted to crawl into my own cocoon and never come out. A cocoon would make me feel safe, where I would not have to pretend I was okay when I was so far from it.

It was not working out with my job either. Being a teacher requires commitment, patience, dedication, and motivation. I tried so hard to refocus, but my normal drive and determination were gone. The insurmountable grief, coupled with the knee pain I was still in physical therapy for, left me with little, if anything, to give to my students. I knew they deserved more and it made me feel even worse that I could not deliver. I was physically and emotionally bankrupt. I was at the point of crash and burn. I knew I had to do something. I put in a request for a leave of absence and without hesitation, it was granted. The school district I worked for had been so incredibly understanding and patient throughout all of Randy's illness as well as with my own surgeries. They were doing the same now with this. I was grateful to them then and still am to this day.

The time off allowed me to heal physically. It also gave me time to attempt to discover what my *new normal* was going to look like. I didn't want a new normal but I had no choice. This was my life now and I knew I could not stay in this state. I knew I had to return to work at the end of my leave. Staying home was not an option for me.

I am an author and had been writing a young adult novel at the time of Randy's death. It was close to completion. I used to read him chapters and he would tell me what he liked or did not like about each one. He was excited for me to get this book published. He was very proud of me for having had my first book published. I knew I had to finish this second one. However, there was a problem. Writing was extremely difficult for me to take on again. My head was still in such a fog and I saw no way out. The grief that consumed me made it nearly impossible to function, much less to be creative. Writer friends suggested that I start a blog, just writing about my feelings. They thought it might help me get back into the writing mode. I hesitated at first but eventually tried it. Most of my blog posts were about what I was experiencing and what was happening in our family. Because I relied on faith a lot through my journey, my posts also included a spiritual viewpoint of things. My writer friends were correct. Over time it became cathartic. I wanted to finish that book and I wanted to dedicate it to him. Ironically, the premise of the book had to do with a boy dealing with the death of his father. Never in my wildest dreams could I have imagined the book having a couple of parallel storylines when I first started writing it. I completed the book and submitted it to the same publishing company who had published my first one. They wanted it and offered a contract. The day my copy of that book arrived in the mail was a day with dual tears. I was weeping with joy to see it in print, but I was also weeping with sadness that Randy was not with me to share in the event. The dedication in the book was to him, just as I wanted.

I read more self-improvement books during my time off as well. This time I was reading about overcoming grief. One of the books had a workbook to write alongside as I read the chapters. I gained bits and pieces of insight from each of the books I read. Things remained bleak though. There was a veil of darkness covering me. I did not see things in the same light anymore. This would have been a good time to visit family out of state and visit with local friends to occupy my time, but I did not feel like it. I still did not want to be around people unless I had to. Some days were okay and other times, I wanted to stay in bed and be at home alone and wish once more for that cocoon. Grief was ugly and painful, and it was not my friend. I wanted it gone, but it just would not leave.

One thing that became perfectly clear to me was just how short life was. I knew never to let the sun go down while being upset with any loved ones. I knew to say, "I love you" often to people I loved so they never had to wonder once I was gone myself. Luckily, that was not a regret with Randy. We repeated that sentiment several times every day. It was the last thing we told each other every night before going to sleep.

As days turned into weeks, it was time to end my leave of absence and return to work. During that time, I felt stronger physically and I was having more days of feeling somewhat better emotionally. I knew two things. I knew I still had a very long way to go in my healing process. I was not anywhere near being fully okay yet, although I became good at hiding it. I did not want people walking on eggshells around me anymore. In addition, at this point in time, I felt in my mind and in my heart, I was still Randy's wife and I was still very much married.

"The way you grieve may be different from mine, but it doesn't mean your heart is less wounded."

Peggy Bell

SECTION TWO
SOUND FAMILIAR?

My story does not end here. I will pick up on the rest later. I have included this section to share some of the difficulties I faced when unexpectedly finding myself a widow. As you know, losing a spouse changes every part of you. Your family dynamic changes, and so do your circle of friends, your finances, your job situation, your self-worth, your confidence, and your sense of security to name a few. I, like you, experienced those and more, along with the heartache and pain. I cried myself to sleep more times than I care to remember, and I pretended things were fine when it was so far from the truth. Some areas were especially difficult to cope with. You may recognize yourself in these areas as well. Maybe you have felt things I did not mention. I did include some areas that I found helpful in my grieving process. I hope you might find them helpful as well.

****

Grieving Within The Family- On the day we met with the funeral director to make arrangements, he gave all of us a small piece of advice. To this day I remain thankful that he shared this. He told us that everyone sitting in that room would grieve differently. It did not mean that one person's grief was better or worse than anyone else's was. It did not mean that one loved him more or less because of the way they chose to grieve. We didn't know it then but it was indeed so true. I felt the need to visit the cemetery very often for at least the first two years. I wanted to be there every day, but some days I could not because of my knee surgery. One daughter visited whenever she could. Another just could not go to the cemetery at all. It was too upsetting for her. We accepted that in each other without judgment. We did share the need as well as the desire to speak of him often. We shared stories and memories. We laughed a lot and we cried a lot at the beginning. The memories were painful at first and made us miss him even more but it did not stop us. We still speak of him often to this very day. His memories are alive and will remain in us always. Now my two grandchildren know about their "Papa" and what kind of man he was. They also know some of his funny stories and they laugh about it.

A Feeling Of Numbness- Chances are, at the onset you felt numb about everything. You even had trouble concentrating. That was the case for me. I cried a lot but even then reality wasn't sinking in because I couldn't concentrate and just felt numb. When there were people around me, I saw them and spoke to them. I even appreciated them being with me but it was like I was on autopilot, just going through the motions. I could not tell you about the conversation.

Forgetfulness/Distractions- Along with the numbness I felt, I was constantly forgetting things and was more distracted. I knew not to trust myself to remember important dates, appointments, or errands. I had to rely on family members to remember for me. If you have family or friends who can do that for you, it will really help. Now with the latest technology there are other ways to get reminders that would not have to involve anyone else. You may have heard the term, *widow's brain* or *widow's fog*. I had a full-blown case of it.

"Trying to sleep when your soul is shattered is like trying to count the teardrops that fall from your eyes because of it. Both are nearly impossible."

Peggy Bell

Disrupted Sleep Patterns- You may find that sleep is as difficult for you as it was for me. Trying to sleep when your soul is shattered is like trying to count the teardrops that fall from your eyes because of it. Both are nearly impossible. All I wanted to do was hug my husband's pillow and cry. We used to cuddle and share quiet time before turning over and falling asleep each night. We never turned over

without saying, "I love you." I was alone now and missing our quiet time. I was no longer able to hear him tell me those special three words. Eventually I fell asleep from total exhaustion but then was awake an hour or so later with the pain returning. It was a vicious cycle. Some people receive medication to help them sleep. I was not able to take it. For some of you, maybe all you might want to do is sleep. Just know that disrupted sleep patterns are common. It is not that unusual for someone to start having nightmares. It did not happen to me, but it did happen to women I know.

Friends- Sometimes friends or family members want to help but do not know how. They feel helpless. Besides remembering appointments etc. as previously mentioned, sometimes just having them close by may help. I believe friends are blessings sent to you when just trying to function requires too much effort. Let them be the shoulder to cry on, the ears for listening, or at least let them be a voice on the other end of the phone call. Do not be afraid or hesitant to ask for help. This is something they can do for you and probably want to do. Let them. I never wanted to impose on anyone so I did not reach out to friends at first. In hindsight, I wish I had. Eventually, I did have to ask for help with things. It was then I realized most good friends and family really *do* want to help but just don't know how or even what to say for that matter. If you need help with even the smallest things, just ask. I am sure there is someone willing and wanting to be there for you.

Fear- It can be frightening to know that your life has been turned inside out, not sure where you are headed or what you are supposed to do. The direction in which you thought you were going has come to an abrupt halt. All I can remember was taking this new life just one hour at a time. It was all I could do. A whole day was too much for me to think about at first. My emotional state was too fragile. I got through an hour and worked on the next. That's how my days played out early on in this process. I certainly could not think about the days ahead or my future at that point. Eventually, as time progressed, it started to improve and I could handle things in larger time increments. It is okay to feel that way. Sometimes it is too much to try to take it all in at once. Feel proud of yourself for getting through an hour at a time. It's one hour you may not have been able to get through just days before.

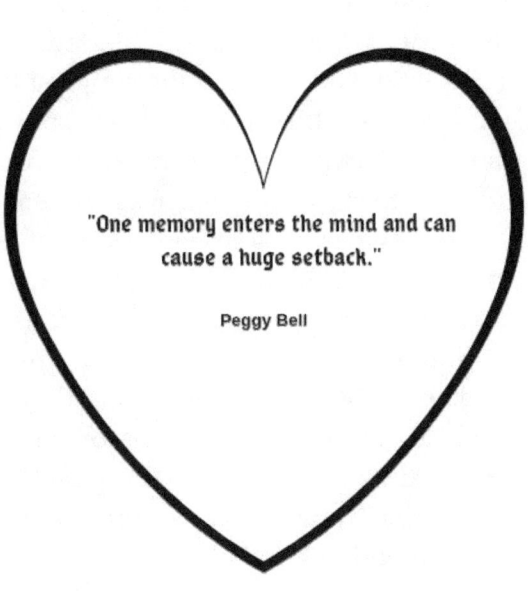

"One memory enters the mind and can cause a huge setback."

Peggy Bell

Setbacks- Talk about naïve! I actually believed I would grieve for a while with each day getting better until things eventually returned to *normal.* I thought I was a strong person and had dealt with tough issues before. I was so wrong on this one. I did not have a clue how painful this would be. Just as I stated before, I was able to handle more as time progressed. What I did not expect were the setbacks that I came to call, *grief eruptions.* I could have a few good days that would make me believe I was on the road towards a full recovery. Then something would happen to make me feel like I was right back where I started. It was so discouraging. Sometimes it was just the simplest things that would cause it. It was like trying to climb a rope to get out of a dark hole and right when you are making progress, you slip down and have to start over. Setbacks are real and most people have them. Grief is a rollercoaster of emotional energy. Keep that in mind and do not be too hard on yourself if or when that happens to you. Just be assured that it is common and try not to beat yourself up for it. We sometimes tend to be our own worst critic don't we? The setbacks will subside in time. They will become farther apart and less painful as time goes on. You will come to hold your own on that proverbial rope and crawl out of that dark hole on your own and in your own time.

"Our anniversary was the one day set
aside for just the two of us."

Peggy Bell

The Firsts- The first holidays, the first anniversary, the first birthday are all hard to go through. If you have had to face them so far, I'm sure you will agree. Randy's birthday was a month after his death so that was an early one for me. These "firsts" trigger so many memories. We were used to having traditions in our family. I knew it would be extremely difficult to have these days come, knowing that a main artery of the family was forever gone. We decided beforehand that we would change the traditions and make new ones. We would remember the old ones but start fresh. It helped some but it was still very hard. My daughter's wedding was right after New Year's Day, four and a half months after his passing. It was another special day for our family and as I stated earlier, it was nice but bittersweet. It was not anything like we had envisioned. Our first wedding anniversary without him was nine months later. That particular "first" was such a difficult one for me because it was so personal. Our anniversary was the one day set aside for just the two of us. We usually went out for a nice dinner. Sometimes we took an out of town trip. Many times he gave me flowers. After he passed, I went to the cemetery for each anniversary. I felt closer to him when I did. Instead of getting flowers *from him*, I brought flowers *for him* to the cemetery. How I wished it didn't have to be that way. It was my reality now and I still hated it. My suggestion is, if you haven't already done so, to try to make new traditions with your family in the way that you can still celebrate those special days. Though still painful, it does help some. Trying to do the same thing without your loved one being present may cause you to miss them even more and be unable to see past the huge hole that was left. The pain and the loss on regular days are bad enough. I wanted to ease the sorrow on those days however I could, not only for myself, but for my daughters as well.   In addition, now that he was gone, I wanted to end the traditions we once had and cherish them as treasured memories.

People Move On- We had many people drop in from the first day of Randy's passing. They brought condolences, lunch, fellowship and prayers. This went on for about a week or so. Then it stopped. People have lives of their own. I certainly get it. That being said, this is also the time when the real loneliness sets in. You find yourself alone in the house with a disturbing presence of silence surrounded by so many things that remind you of your spouse. It is not a good mixture at this point. It was funny to me in an odd sort of way because for so many years, being a teacher and then having children at home, I often wished to have some silent time to myself. I found out that it is not all it's cracked up to be. In other words, be careful what you wish for, right? I can only suggest that you try to occupy your mind with things other than memories or reliving the loss. However, I know it's not easy to do when you are consumed with grief.

People Mean Well- I know that people mean well and I certainly didn't let hard feelings develop because of it, but some things that were said to me made me annoyed and sometimes even angry. I heard, "I know how you feel" from people who had never lost a spouse. The truth is, no, they didn't know how I felt then or even now. Unless you have been thrown into this club that no one wants to belong, then you really don't know how I feel. When it was time for my daughter's wedding, I heard, "Don't be sad. He will be with you." I knew what they meant, but I was very sad because I wanted him there with us physically, walking my daughter down the aisle, celebrating a night he was so looking forward to having. For him to be there in spirit only was not what I wanted. So hearing that comment repeatedly by numerous people did not console me in the least. Another great one was, "It's time to let this go and move on." Says who? Since when is there an expiration on grief? Again, this usually came from people who never experienced such loss. As I said, they meant well. They were not saying it to be cruel. They were friends and family. I just had to keep reminding myself of this. I wondered if I had ever said those things in the past myself, only trying to be consoling and helpful. Chances are I probably had. Try not to let people's well intentions get you down. You have enough to deal with. Sometimes people just feel helpless and are at a loss for comforting words. What they do not realize is if they would come out and say just that, we would understand and appreciate their honesty.

Another Scenario- If you aren't spending each day crying, people may wonder and question if you truly loved your spouse because you should be feeling sadder than you are. This never happened to me personally but I know some who have experienced this. They felt guilty because of those comments. We all grieve differently and until people go through it themselves, they truly do not understand that concept. If you are that type of person who doesn't cry easily or internalizes your emotions, do not let others upset you or make you feel guilty. Only you know what you are feeling and that is what really matters.

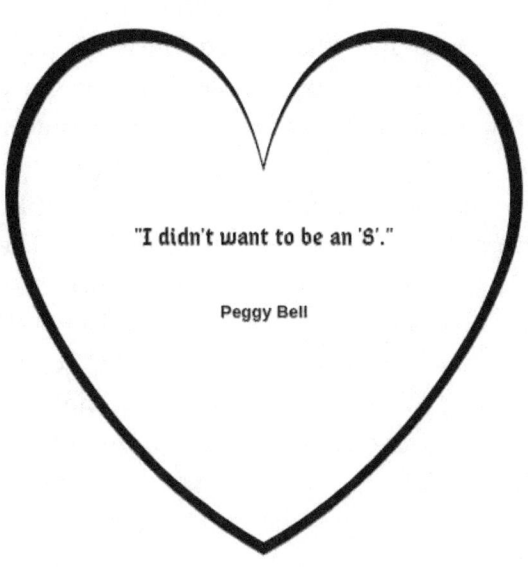

"I didn't want to be an 'S'."

Peggy Bell

Being An "S"- I remember this one incident so well. A little over a year after losing Randy I was enrolling for an upcoming retreat at our church. I had gone in the afternoon. The church was open for those who wanted to drop in and sign up. There was no one there went I went. I started filling out the paperwork. Then I got to the part that asked me to circle my marital status. The choices were: "M" for married, "S" for single, or "D" for divorced. At that very instant the walls around me came crashing down and I felt like I was punched in the gut. I was still married. I mean, I knew I was a widow, but to me, that word meant I was a married woman who had lost my spouse. That was my definition anyway. I had taken off my wedding rings but had replaced them with an anniversary band I bought. It symbolized to me what I felt our marriage was. It was a simple, yet strong bond, with a never-ending love for Randy. The people at church knew I was widowed. They had been a big support for me. So there was my dilemma. I couldn't really circle the M because I knew what they meant by M. I certainly wasn't a D. But, I didn't WANT to be an S! I had not asked to be an S! It was not my choice to be one! I remember I just stood there, with anxiety consuming me. How could a task so simple in others' eyes get the best of me this way? I walked around the back of church, totally distraught over one darn letter! I just couldn't do it. I couldn't circle the S. I was not ready. I went back to the table, took a deep breath, added a W for widowed, circled it, placed it in the box and left, feeling emotionally exhausted. To some, it may seem like this was such an easy thing to do. I could have written that from the start or left it blank because they all knew me. They would have understood. For me, it was so much more than that. For the very first time since my husband's death, I began to question my marital status. I realized that what I believed and felt in my heart was not how society viewed it.

Fifth Wheel- Having been married for thirty years, we did most things either with family or with friends. Our close friends were all married. When I finally did start to get out of the house more, I felt uncomfortable being with our longtime friends now. Everyone was with his or her spouse except for me. They were very gracious and certainly did not make me feel uncomfortable, but it was just me. I felt empty, like something was not right any longer. That's because something wasn't right. Randy wasn't with me. He was the clown and the entertainer in our group of friends. Now that was gone and it made me miss him even more. I stayed away for a long time, though kept in touch by phone call or text messages. Today, I am able to visit these friends again and it is fine because the dynamics have changed. Time has progressed. There are grandchildren, sons and daughters-in law. It's no longer just couples. I have had widowed friends who have had no problem continuing the outings with their own close friends. I personally think it's great and hope you can do the same. I just felt uncomfortable, and personally, it hurt too much. In time, it did get better. True friends understand and will always welcome you back with open arms when the time is right for you.

Dreams- During the early part of my grief, I went to bed at night crying and hoping if I fell asleep that I would at least dream of him. That way he could be with me again physically even though it was only in my dreams. I longed to be able to speak with him again, hug him and laugh with him. I missed him so much. I did dream of him on occasion but not nearly as much as I would have liked. It didn't seem to be those types of dreams I longed for though. He would enter my dreams in what seemed to be very briefly, taking part in whatever was happening and then he was gone. There was never alone time in my dreams the way I wanted. I am no expert in the dream field; not even a little bit. I just know what I would have loved to dream about and what I actually did dream. He still does enter my dreams sometimes, though not very often anymore.

Cleaning Out The Closet and Drawers - One of the difficult tasks came when I took his clothes out of his side of our closet and in our dresser. Actually, looking back on it, I did this rather quickly. I did it when I was on leave from work. I viewed it as helping others who may need clothes. It was being put to good use. In hindsight, I wish I would have kept more pieces than I did. Today, people are able to make blankets, pillows, stuffed animals and the like with a loved one's clothing. I did not know of anyone doing that back then. Had I kept more of his clothing I could have done it now. I have friends who have never removed their husband's clothing. It still hangs where it did while they were alive. I don't think there is a right or wrong way to think about this. Just make sure the decision is yours and you don't feel pressured to do or not do anything you are not comfortable doing.

Remembering Him- I longed to hear my husband's voice again. I wanted to smell his scent, and I wanted to remember his touch. I kept a bottle of his cologne in my closet. I sprayed some on his pillow case. Sometimes I sprayed it in the air just so I could take in the scent. After some time I started to forget the sound of his voice. I found that very upsetting and quite painful. My daughter found two voicemails on her phone from him. It was such a gift to have her find those. We made sure they were preserved. I was grateful for two out of three. But what would I give to feel his touch just one more time! To feel his arms around me or to touch his hand was something I desperately longed for.

Your New Role – In my case, Randy was ill for about the last ten years of our marriage. As time went on, his illness progressed, becoming dependent on oxygen and a wheelchair. In the last two years, he was no longer driving or working. I worked during the day teaching, came home and at least two or three days a week he had doctor appointments. This meant rushing home from work, loading him, the oxygen tank, and his wheelchair into the van and getting to his appointments on time. Then it meant coming home from the appointments and trying to get a quick dinner prepared. Many times we picked up take out because we got out of the appointments so late. My role in life was to be wife, mother, teacher, driver and caretaker. When he passed, suddenly I was no longer wife, driver, or caretaker. Soon, my daughters were out of the house so I wasn't needed as a mother the way they needed me when they were young or even still living at home. I began to question my own identity. Who was I now, and what was my new role in life? I found myself with time on my hands; too much time. What was I to do with it? I regretted all the times I complained about being so busy and not being able to catch a break or have a minute to myself. It was another, *be careful what you wish for* lesson for me. Unfortunately, I was learning the hard way.

Both Roles- A few things starting breaking in the house not long after losing Randy. Household matters such as these were always his responsibility, which made me happy. I knew the basic difference between a hammer and a wrench. I just had no desire to use either. Now I knew I had to have an attitude adjustment. I could not call a repairperson for simple things, and I could not always call on friends. The first thing to break was something inside of the toilet tank in the guest bathroom. I took a picture of it, went to the hardware store, and showed them. They told me it was an easy fix. They showed me what I needed and told me how to do it. I went home, grabbed the correct tool, and proceeded to work. Presto! I fixed it in a very short while and I never had trouble with it after that. I was very proud of myself (as well as surprised). Other things needed repairs over time. Some were simple and some not quite so much. In the case of those big repairs, I had the repairperson's number on speed dial. Hopefully, you are better at handling repairs than I was. If you aren't, put your repairperson's number on speed dial too. I had other things to do besides repairs. Some of them included making sure the lawn was taken care of, preparing the house and outdoor shrubbery for winter, paying bills again since he had taken over this task when he started staying home, taking out the trash and keeping the car maintained.

"It's funny how hearing a certain song on the radio or even seeing a movie can trigger memories and emotions that race to take up space, front and center, in our hearts or in our minds."

Peggy Bell

Triggers - It's funny how hearing a certain song on the radio or seeing a movie can trigger memories and emotions that race to take up space, front and center, in our hearts and in our minds. It takes us back to that special time. We relive the memories as vividly as if they just happened. For some of you, maybe they have indeed just happened. For others, it was long ago. Either way, some people are left feeling sad and missing that person when the song is heard or the movie begins. What may have started as a relatively good day has now taken you back to that empty, lonely place. It's one of those *grief eruptions* we spoke of. It is the slip of that rope. On the other hand, sometimes people are left feeling better for having relived the memory of that person, even if for a short while. It all depends on how the trigger affects you. For me, now that time has passed, it's easier to hear the songs that take me back. They make me smile. Some songs even make me laugh when I think about the situation or memory that surrounds that song. On the other hand, some songs I still turn off when I hear them. They are negative triggers that I will not allow to enter my mind. I will not go there. I'm not much of a movie person so that hasn't been much of an issue. Randy liked the "blood and guts" kind of movies. If I was going to watch one, I wanted it to be a comedy or a romantic movie. We did not go to movies very much because of it (insert smile).

Major Life Changes- People told me not to make major changes or decisions in my life for at least the first year. I would just nod, not understanding what they meant by that. At the time of Randy's death, making big changes was not even on my radar. I could barely get through the day. I wasn't about to try and make big life changes. I tended to legal matters, but they were not big decisions to make. They were made beforehand and were part of his will. The strange thing was, that even after almost two years, I *thought* the decisions I was starting to make sounded reasonable. In my mind I was *sure* I was clear headed enough to proceed and decide things for myself and what was best for me. I was wrong. People around me saw it, but I could not. Maybe that was part of the journey; thinking you are better when you really aren't quite there yet. So heed that advice and take it from me that there is truth in it. Looking back on it now, I wasn't ready at the time to decide on some of the things I was trying to do. That was the scary part. I really thought I was. Before you decide to make big life changes, you may want to run it by a family member or close friend. Choose someone who has no stake in the matter and all they want is to see a good outcome that is truly in your best interest.

"There are other things besides losing our spouse for which we grieve."

Peggy Bell

Finances- Some of the things I had to look at rather quickly was what cash we had on hand, how much debt I was looking at, what would be taken care of by insurance coverage, and how his absence of income would affect my life going forward. You will want to tend to this as well. If you still cannot think clearly, ask a trusted friend or family member to help you. Just be cautious whom you ask for help. I do not say this to be mean but only as a word of caution. Know without a doubt that loved ones are acting only in *your* own best interest and not in their own. I know women who were too trusting and they found themselves in an unexpected mess.

Grieving Your Future and What's Not To Be- Losing a spouse is incredibly difficult. I don't think anyone disputes that. However, we grieve for other things as well. One of them is for the plans that may have been made for the future and will never come to fruition. In my case, we used to talk often of our retirement years and what we planned to do when we became empty nesters. When he died, so did all of our plans. I could still do some of them, but he wouldn't be there so it wasn't the same. I grieved for that loss as well. It was the future that was never meant to be. You may find yourself grieving for your future as you imagined it or some other plan that was not meant to be. I have since learned not to rely on the future. I have learned to treasure the past but live in the present. It's the only thing I somewhat have control over.

Seeking Help- Sometimes things are very difficult to overcome. If you feel as though you need to speak with a professional, then do it. Please do not see it as a sign of weakness. Do not see it as needing to be prescribed unwanted medication or in long-term treatment. It can be very helpful if you think you need it. Support groups can be beneficial as well. The funeral home we went through for Randy's passing offered a support group. Nearby churches offered them as well. There are also support groups on social media. I fact, I have one myself which I will mention later on. There are counselors and therapists if you feel you need someone from the medical community. There are also life coaches who can help you get through the grief and on to finding your new normal. Again, do not do this alone if you feel that you are just not able to deal with it all.

Close Family- My parents and siblings called and checked on my daughters and me often. We lived in a different state than they did so they could not just drop in for a short visit, but they made sure we were okay. I was very blessed and still am to call them family. I hope you have a close family member or members as well. If you don't, sometimes friends can be the closest thing to family, and in some instances, even better.

In-laws – The relationship you will maintain with your in-laws will probably depend upon the relationship you had with them before your loss. Randy had two sisters who were each married with a family of her own. I considered them family before, and I still consider them family today, even though I have remarried. I remain close to all of them, and they were one hundred percent supportive of me marrying again. I consider myself very fortunate.

Jealousy- It is not unusual to see other couples holding hands or being close and feeling jealous or envious of them. It seems unfair that you wanted the same for yourself but it was taken from you. Some may even feel anger about it. For a long time, when I looked at other happy couples enjoying themselves, I just felt sad for missing out on more of that. I didn't feel jealous or angry. That's not to say you won't. Many women do feel that way.

Physical Health- It is just as important to take care of your physical health as it is your mental state. I know eating properly, or eating at all for that matter, may be the last thing you want to think about early on, but it is important. Also, keep in mind that exercise releases endorphins, which elevate the mood so you may want to give it a try. I couldn't exercise because of my knee situation except for physical therapy. There aren't many things that completely cut off my appetite, but I have to say that grief was one thing that did it early on.

Prescribed Medication- Drugs-Alcohol – We all want the pain to go away. Can I get an "Amen" on that? Remember I said I just wished I could crawl up into my own cocoon and stay there? Your doctor may prescribe medicine for you if he thinks you need it. If he does prescribe it, then take it, but only take it as prescribed. Don't abuse legal or illegal drugs or even alcohol for that matter. It may numb you for a while, but you will only come out of it still depressed. It is quite possible that if you abuse it for a while, you will find yourself with even more problems than grief. The last thing you want to do is create more problems at this point. Keep in mind that some of these act as a depressant also. Do you really want to be more depressed? Again, to be clear, I am not speaking about prescribed medications taken properly, but rather abuse of drugs or alcohol. I myself, never had a problem with it, but I know women who have. It made the grief recovery so much harder because they had to also check into rehabilitation for the substance abuse.

Journal Writing- I strongly suggest you keep a journal through your grief journey to write down your thoughts and feelings. Through the heartache, it will be difficult to see progress. After writing in it for a while, you will be able to look back and see how far you have come and what you still have to work on. I did this, except that I did it through my blog. I looked back on it years later and was amazed how low I was and how far I had come.

SECTION THREE
MY STORY: YEARS LATER

After nearly three years, I started recognizing my old self. I was having more good days than bad. I could remember the past without getting so sad and emotional. I could hear Randy's name and feel thankful for the years we had together. Sure, I would have liked many more years together, but that was no longer my reality and I had to come to terms with it. Over time, I started the transition to a new part of my life. My cocoon was beginning to go through its own personal metamorphosis. I was learning my *new normal*. I felt more comfortable getting out and being amongst friends. Once I did, I heard a strange but familiar sound. It was the sound of my own laughter returning. It was weird to hear at first because it had been so long since I laughed with friends, but it felt good and I knew I wanted to continue to feel that way. I knew I was ready to move on, accept my new normal for what it was, and carry on with the rest of my life. I realized early on just how short life was and not to take my life for granted. I knew I could no longer love or live in the past. I knew that for a long time actually, but I just had not been ready to take those steps. It was one of those things that my mind knew but my heart would not allow.

One thing I want you to understand is that it didn't happen overnight. Did you notice the title of this section? As much as I wanted to move on, laugh, and enjoy life, there was still a part of me that felt *guilty* for wanting to do so. I was hesitant. I felt it would somehow send a message to the world that I didn't really love my husband if I moved on; that trying to be happy again would mean I only loved him a little. The fact is, that couldn't have been farther from the truth. It was *because* I loved him so much that I knew I couldn't remain in that cocoon state. As I mentioned earlier, Randy was a man who loved life and loved to laugh. I came to realize that I was not honoring his memory by being a recluse or by crying constantly. I knew he wouldn't approve of me continuing to live that way. I knew if he had the chance to talk to me, he would ask me what I thought I was doing by living that way. He would tell me I couldn't spend the rest of my life being the way I was. He would also tell me to dry the tears, move on, and enjoy my life. And there was something else I knew he would tell me because I believe it to be so. He would tell me he was happy where he was, healed from all his pain and illness. I realized there was a better way to honor him, and at the same time, it would be better for me as well. That's what I chose to do. I stopped worrying about what the world might or might not think of me for moving on. In fact, my family and closest friends gave me their full support.

When the veil of darkness (grief) was lifted, I began to see things more clearly. The old cliché,

What doesn't kill you makes you stronger, rang true in my case. I realized how much stronger of a person I became. It wasn't because I wanted to be stronger. It was because I was forced to do so. It was the only option. I was more independent. I was more self-confident, and I was more appreciative of life. Figuratively speaking, I was given the gift of a new heart. The old one that bled out and withered never revived. That heart was for loving Randy. It always was and always would be. It was "buried" with him. I had a new heart now, different from the original, to move on in a different direction of my life. I was no longer the exact woman I used to be. Grief reminded me of the small stuff I used to stress about that was really nonsense and it taught me to no longer worry about things I cannot control. I learned to appreciate each day I was given and all the little things that are part of it. Grief changed me in other ways too. It wasn't in bad ways. It was just in different ways.

Eventually I sold our family home and moved into a small apartment. For some people, they decide to stay in the home. They want to keep it because it was the home they had as a family. They want to preserve the memories and make more. For others, including myself, we see it as the home we shared when we were together as a family. However, that family dynamic no longer existed. My husband was gone, and my daughters left home to be on their own. The house was too large for just me. It made me sad to look around and see what once was, but never to be again. I wanted to always remember and treasure the memories that we made there together. It was not an easy decision to make. I toyed with the idea for a while. I actually put it on the market to sell and changed my mind. Some time after I put it up for sale again, and this time it sold within twenty-four hours! The day I locked the door for the last time was highly emotional. I sat in my car in the driveway, while many memories flooded my mind. Many tears fell too, but I knew I had made the right decision for me. I was ready to make a fresh start for myself. I wanted new beginnings. Once I was moved and settled into my apartment, I was excited to know that I really did have a life ahead of me.

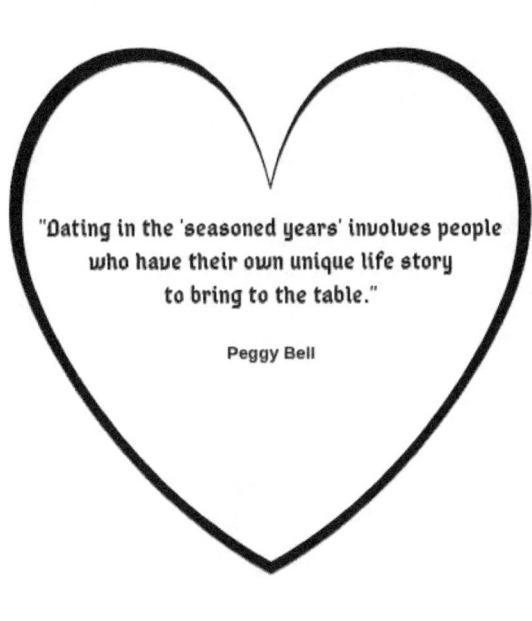

"Dating in the 'seasoned years' involves people
who have their own unique life story
to bring to the table."

Peggy Bell

SECTION FOUR
DATING AGAIN

I found myself ready for male companionship again. I must admit though, when that thought first entered my mind, I blocked it out as quickly as it came. Guilt consumed me even more now for allowing myself to think it. One possibility for the guilt may have been the fact that we had never discussed moving forward after one of us was gone. I wish we had. I blame myself for that. Randy was ill for years and would bring up things about him passing before I did and I would just blow it off. I guess I didn't want to upset him or show him that I also believed he would go before I would. Maybe I was partially in denial. I remember going to the cemetery before I did start dating again. I actually talked to him and explained my feelings, my plans, my guilt, and how I wished he would have told me how he felt about me moving on. I remember *asking for his approval*. And I remember getting that approval in a way that would only come from Randy.

Dating was so awkward at first. I hadn't been on a date in 30 plus years. It was so different from dating back in my teens and twenties. People didn't meet the same way they did back then. It was new and even somewhat confusing. Getting ready for my first date was surreal and almost comical. Remember how you felt as a teen getting ready for your first date ever? That was me; excited and nervous at the same time, wondering if we would have anything to talk about. Thankfully, it went well. We met at a restaurant. It was nice to go to dinner and share mature conversation, very different from the very first date scenario way back when.

Dating in the *seasoned years* involves people who have their own unique life story to bring to the table. Some are divorced and bitter, while some are divorced and better. Some are widowed. Most have children and even grandchildren. Some have never been married, though I did not date anyone in that case. It wouldn't have mattered. It just happened that I didn't. It felt good to be out there again, enjoying life. I kept dating, and through the process, rekindled old friendships and met some real nice gentlemen, who to this day, still consider to be my friends.

I met one in particular. He was a widower after a thirty year marriage as well. The rest as they say, "is history". As I write this, we have been married for two years. The funny thing is his name. Are you ready for it? His name is....Randy. No, I am not kidding. It wasn't planned that way. Trust me when I say it was pure coincidence. I was introduced to him by his nickname. I always did say my God has a sense of humor. Or either he knows how bad I am at remembering names and wanted to help me out (insert smile).

The life I had in my first marriage remains a treasure with the fondest of memories. My current husband understands it because he holds the memories of his late wife in the same way. There is no jealously. We speak openly about both of them and tell stories about them. We know that's a part of our own history that will always remain with us. We "get it". Maybe that is an advantage of marrying a widower? I have no idea, but it works well for us.

SECTION FIVE
STAGES OF GRIEF- REAL OR NOT?

You may have heard there are stages of grief we all go through. If you google it, you might see there are five stages. Another article may say there are seven stages. Still others say there are really no stages at all. Perhaps grief consists of emotions in no particular order and not everyone may experience all of them. Although I am no doctor, and I don't even play one on TV, I choose to believe the latter. In fact, science is acknowledging that more today than they did before, realizing the so-called "stages" of grief were misinterpreted. Grief is not linear, nor does it follow a timeline.

When I first became a widow, I heard about five stages of grief. I looked at them, but they did not all pertain to me. One stage or emotion I did not experience was anger. I wasn't angry at Randy, at God, or anyone else. I couldn't be angry at Randy. He hadn't asked for his illness. I wasn't angry at God either. If anything, I was grateful that Randy was no longer suffering. My own personal faith told me that he was healed after death. That actually brought me some comfort. Your spiritual faith, your guidance, or your direction may be different from mine. I speak only for myself. I know there are many women who do experience anger. Sometimes there are lots of it. Sometimes it is because of the circumstances surrounding the death.

Another emotion some women go through is bargaining. Randy's death, even though he was ill, was sudden and unexpected. There was no time to bargain. I don't think I would have even if there were time. Neither did I bargain to take the grief away. I knew I had to go through it to heal.

We experience many emotional parts of our grief in similar ways. Still, there are differences in the way we choose to handle or get through our grief journey. There is no date on the calendar that states our grief time is up and we must move forward. Some people are ready to move forward after a short while. Some people go years before being ready. Still, others wonder if they will ever be ready. Let it be your decision and no one else's. Don't let anyone pressure you or make you feel bad because you haven't moved on yet or that you are moving forward too quickly. In my nonmedical opinion, grief is just a jumbled up mess that comes and goes. It is the price we pay for loving someone as much as we did.

Know that it is okay to move on when you are ready to do so. It is going to be a gut instinct you feel with a strong desire to put the sad, heart wrenching days behind you. You will be ready to discover and start living your *new normal.* I sometimes refer to this as your *true north.* Don't be like I was and worry that the world might judge you for the decision you make. Only you know what's in your heart. Only you know what your marriage truly meant to you and always will. Don't let anyone diminish what your marriage meant to you because you want to move forward.

I personally believe we are not made to be alone. We as humans are social by nature. The loneliness I felt was not fun. My life alone was pretty miserable. Being alone and not socializing with friends or family for long periods of time is not a healthy way to live. I suggest you contact your friends and ask to go to dinner, coffee, or to a movie. Chances are they have already asked you and you turned them down. Consider contacting them now. Start with small steps. Find groups you can join in your area that share your same interests. Please don't misunderstand me. I am in no way implying that moving on means you have to meet someone else and date or marry. That may or may not be for you, now or ever. Moving forward means just what it says. It's grabbing hold of that rope and finally making your way out of the dark hole. Moving forward means that you see things more clearly than you have seen them in a long time. Moving forward means you want to live the rest of your life. Moving forward means you look at your future now with more hope than dread. And lastly, in my opinion, moving forward means you are honoring your husband's memory in a special way; to go on living.

SECTION SIX
LEAVE A LASTING MEMORY

There are other ways in which you could honor your husband and leave a lasting memory, not just for yourself but for others to honor him as well.

- You can consider setting up an annual scholarship in his name at a local high school. The amount can be as low or as high as you'd like. It can be given to a high school senior going into the same vocation or career field that your husband was in.

- On his birthday or anniversary of his death, you could donate a book to a different library each year. It could be a public or school library. Librarians can usually put a bookplate on the inside cover stating who the book is in memory of. The subject could be about a hobby he liked, something work related, or just anything that relates to him.

- You could also donate a book each year to other places besides libraries. Some suggestions are retirement homes, children's hospitals, cancer treatment centers, and hospice centers. You could buy your own bookplates or write something inside yourself about why this book was donated.

- Plant a tree in the park, in the city, or at your own home. Some will require permission from the city or town. Some may allow you to add a plaque.

- Buy gifts on the special day and donate them to nursing homes.

- Plant a memory garden in your yard.

- Donate a bench in his memory to a park or school. You could have an inscription attached to it.

- You could have a butterfly release each year with a gathering of family and friends.

- You could hire an artist to paint a mural on a wall of your house (any size) to represent his personality.

- You could give to charities in his name each year.

These are just some ideas. They vary in price range of what it would cost. You may be able to think of more on your own. It usually makes us feel better when we give to others. Giving to others in this way lets us know that your husband is being honored and remembered, not only by you, but also by others who may have never heard his name.

"The veil of grief is lifted and the world around me is colorful once again."

Peggy Bell

SECTION SEVEN
AGE IS JUST A NUMBER

I retired from teaching after thirty-eight years. My knees continued to deteriorate and standing all day became too much for me. I tried staying home and enjoying the retired life. It was good for a while, but I soon realized it was not me. It's funny because I had always longed for retirement, when I could stay home and do absolutely nothing. Uh, wrong! (for me anyway).

I started writing again. But this time I wanted to change genres. Instead of writing children's books, I wanted to write nonfiction for adults, and I knew what topic I wanted to write. I knew in my heart if I could help women understand grief a little better, it would be worth it. That's when I started writing this book.

Along the way, as I believe God would have it, my calling became much deeper than just writing books. Right before my sixtieth birthday, I became a certified life coach. I decided one of my special niches would be helping widows find their new normal when they felt ready to move forward. I know you're shocked (insert smile). I truly believe we as women go through so many things in our lives. No woman should be stuck in a state of grief. I want to help her. However, as we well know, it has to be when she feels ready and not before.

I invite all widows to join my online support group, Life After Loss For Widows. You will find support and conversations with women in different places along their grief journey. It is a place to go without judgement. I encourage as much interaction in the group as possible. You never know when your story or a few short words can help someone who is having a particularly bad day. You can find contact information on my "About the Author" page.

I want you to know that as difficult as grief is, there can still be life on the other side. It does not matter your age or your circumstance. I called my business, "Live Your Purpose" because I believe that is what life is all about. We need to find out our purpose in life and live it authentically. The tagline for my business is, "Life is Short. Make It Count." I use this tagline because I believe there is so much truth in those six little words. We, more than most people, know just how short life can be. We need to make the best of it. If there is something you have always wanted to do, then do it. If there is something you have always wanted to be, then be it. Do not live with regrets. Do not die with regrets.

I stated at the beginning that I felt we were friends because we share a common bond. I believe that to be true. My sincere wish for all of you is to understand that your grief is real, your grief is common, your grief has no deadline or due date, but your grief should not be a death sentence for you. It is a passage, a season in time, but not a place to stay. You won't ever forget your spouse. You won't get *over* the grief because it truly never ends. You will always miss him. But you can get *through* it. You will one day be able to speak his name and smile about the memories instead of crying. You can move on and you can be happy again. Do you know why? It is because you are stronger than you think you are.

To this day, grief continues to be the most difficult thing I have ever experienced. My veil of grief is lifted, and the world around me is colorful once again. I have completed my personal metamorphosis. It feels good to be alive. I survived grief. And because I did, I know you can survive it too.

ABOUT THE AUTHOR

Peggy Bell lost her husband of thirty years in 2009. She was a widow at age fifty. Although her husband had been ill for years, his death was unexpected. She understands first-hand the gut wrenching heartache a woman experiences when her husband dies. It is her desire to help as many women as possible understand that the feelings, emotions and darkness they are feeling and living in are common. Peggy feels there is a bond between widows. She feels that unless you have experienced it, you cannot understand the depth of the sorrow of the heart.

Peggy is owner of Live Your Purpose. She is a certified life coach, author, speaker, and educator. She has written two children's books, a book for teachers, and journals. She had short stories published in anthologies, written her own blogs, written guest blogs, appeared on podcasts and has visited schools as a guest author.

She lives with her husband in southeast Texas.

Contact Information
www.peggymbell.com

Email : peggybellcoaching@yahoo.com

peggybellwrites@yahoo.com

Facebook: @liveyourpurposelifecoaching

@lifeafterlossforwidows

TOPICS AVAILABLE FOR WORKSHOPS/SPEAKING ENGAGEMENTS

- Overcoming Limiting Beliefs
- Forgiveness
- Authentic Happiness
- Grief Recovery
- Making the Workplace Less Stressful
- Developing A Growth Mindset
- Becoming Your Best Self
- The Hero's Journey- Finding Your Superpower

COACHING OPPORTUNITIES WITH PEGGY

- Individual
- Small Group
- Large Group
- Online Courses (take at own pace)
- Presentations
- Workshops
- Group Retreats (upon request)
- Women's Events
- Breakout Sessions
- Vision 365 (vision board workshops)

OTHER BOOKS BY PEGGY BELL
AVAILABLE AT THIS TIME

Queen of the Castle

Children's chapter book

Ages 6-9

thebookpatch.com

$10.00

Teacher gift book

For all occasions

$5.99

Amazon.com

Happiness Looks Good
On Me:
31 Day Journal
thebookpatch.com
$6.95

I Love Me Because
Journal for Self Worth
thebookpatch.com
$6.29

MORE BOOKS TO BE RELEASED THIS YEAR. STAY IN
TOUCH.

ATTENTION READERS !!

If you would like to receive a free link to download a 10 page adult coloring book on gratitude, please go to my website below and type in the subject or message section, "coloring book". I will email you the link as a token of my own gratitude to you for purchasing this book.

www.peggymbell.com

www.ingramcontent.com/pod-product-compliance
Lightning Source LLC
Chambersburg PA
CBHW020352290526
45785CB00005B/2250